Personal Branding

The Complete Step-by-Step Beginners Guide to Build Your Brand in: Facebook, YouTube, Twitter, and Instagram.
The Best Strategies to Know How to Marketing Yourself, and Dominate Your Market in 2019.

By: Gary Clarke

Introduction

Congratulations on downloading *Personal Branding* and thank you for doing so.

The following chapters will discuss everything that you need to know in order to get started with your own personal branding. Just like working with branding a new product, or a company, a personal brand can help you to become more recognizable to a lot of people around you. Some people are looking to start with this personal branding in order to help them get recognized by their potential employer, and others want to start an online career and become a well-known personality. Either way, you will find that personal branding will be able to help you to get this done.

This guidebook is going to take some time to explore personal branding. We will look at what personal branding is all about, why the right mentality about tis process is so important from the start, the tools that you need to get started on your own personal brand, and some of the steps that you can take in order to get started with the personal branding process. Remember that this is not something that is going to happen overnight. But if you are able to follow the rules in this guidebook, and you are willing to put in the time and the effort, you will find that it can really help make a big difference in your life.

From here, we are going to take a look at some of the other things that you need to do in order to get started with personal branding. We will look at how you can put a good team together, how to pick out the audience you would like promote to, why you should consider having a mentor, and the importance of having a good team to help you get things done.

As we go through this guidebook, we will also explore the tips that you can use in order to promote your personal brand. There are a lot of social media sites that you can use in order to help you to see the best results. We will look at how you can do a personal brand with Facebook, Twitter, YouTube, and more.

Creating a personal brand is a great way for you to work on progressing your career, and many of your other goals. When you are ready to get started on creating your own personal brand in 2019, make sure to check out this guidebook to help you get started.

There are plenty of books on this subject on the market, thanks again for choosing this one! Every effort was made to ensure it is full of as much useful information as possible, please enjoy!

Chapter 1: The Basics of Personal Branding

At some point, you have probably at least heard the term of personal branding in the past. Whether you were reading a self-help book, heard it in the news, or you heard it at work, it seems like everyone is talking about having their own personal brand more and more nowadays. But this brings up the question, what is personal branding and why is it so important?

To keep it simple, a personal brand is going to be when an individual will make up their own titles and careers. And along with this, they will come up with their own personas and personalities to turn themselves into a brand. This can be a big concept that is hard to get a grasp of because it seems to be a bit ridiculous. You may be reading this and wondering, how can someone becomes a brand? Doesn't a brand need to be a product or a company?

When we take a closer look at what exactly a brand is, we are able to see why a personal brand can be something, something that can further an individual in their own career and life. Traditionally, a brand is going to be a uniquely named, uniquely designed entity that will be used in order to sell a single product or a chain of products. Brands will be used in order to sell the products and to make money, often because they successfully created an atmosphere that went with their name and their logo. If this is done in the right manner, these are going to be associated with a highly positive aspect of whatever is being sold.

Let's look at an example of how this is going to work. Most people at least know about the brand Nike, even if they don't personally use it. This company will produce a variety of athletic shoes and other clothing. Over the years, we have come to recognize their signature logo, and we know, without even seeing or hearing the name of the company, who Nike is just by that logo.

Nike has created that logo, and then placed it on every one of their products so that consumers know exactly who the brand is, and whether that is a product that they want to purchase. In addition, Nike doesn't just stop with the logo that they put on their products. They will take the time to endorse some of the famous athletes in order to create a wider branding image, even one that is going to be higher end than some of the others.

All of this, plus more, is going to be done in order to ensure there is an overall impression among the consumers when it comes to that particular brand. This is going to be evident as soon as you ask someone who would be a consumer of that product to summarize the brand with a few words. These could be things like performance enhancing, sleek, top of the line, and more. Or, you may hear that someone likes the product and thinks that Nike, and their line, is cool just because a certain celebrity has worn them.

The only difference between the branding that we just talked about, and personal branding, is that the branding isn't going to be done on a particular product, but it is going to be done for you. You will spend the time doing this same kind of branding on yourself, so that you can sell yourself to others, and get the things that you want.

Your personal brand is the look that you want to show to the rest of the world. You want to make sure that it comes off in a certain way, depending on the outlook that you are trying to get in the end.

Let's say that you are looking to get into a new position. You have finished college, or maybe even been in the field for some time. But now you have decided that it is time to take your skills and expertise and put it to the next level. You can easily work on personal branding in order to portray yourself in a certain way. To do this, you would craft your own persona through your resume, cover letter, emailing, social media sites and more.

You want to make sure that these are all cohesive throughout. This way, no matter how someone finds out about you, they are going to see the image that you want them to. For someone trying to advance themselves in the professional world, or someone who is just out of college trying to get their first career, you would most likely want to set up a personal brand that is professional, confident, and ready to do the job.

But personal branding an work in many other ways as well. You want to make sure that you know what your goal is before you start. If you want to grow your YouTube channel, your persona may be a bit different than the professional trying to grow their career for example. You have to know what you want right from the beginning, and then go for it by creating your own brand and showcasing that to everyone around you.

This guidebook is going to spend some time looking at the basics that you need to know to get started wit your own personal brand, especially in 2019. There are a lot of people who are trying to get the same customers, get the same jobs, and reach the same market. but there are only a few who are successful, and that is because they have mastered the art of personal branding and have done it in a successful manner. So, let's take a look at some of the different things that you can do to help start your own personal brand today.

Chapter 2: How to Have the Right Mentality to Start Your Personal Brand

Building your own personal brand can end up being a tough business. It is going to involve a lot of dedication and hard work, and it can take you some time to work on before you can even see the results. And if you are not in the right space mentally to do this work, personal branding can become even more difficult to handle.

Remember that this personal brand is meant to help you become more attractive, and more marketable, to the consumer. And because of this, you will be opening yourself up to the scorn of the public eye. And if you plan to make some profits from marketing yourself on Instagram and YouTube, you may find that you are going to be attacked by people you don't even know. If you have a consultant or a mentor who is helping you out, you may be reprimanded by them as you work with growing your brand.

You need to remember that it is so important to be in the right mindset from the very beginning. If you are able to do this, it is so much easier for you to make it through all of this, even if you were attacked or things weren't going the way that you would like. Some of the things that you can do to help make sure that your mentality is in the right place includes:

Be positive

When you first go into making your own personal brand, take the time to be positive. This is going to be hard. This is going to take time. and there are going to be some people who are not happy with what you are doing, and who will say mean things online. With all of this coming at you at once, it is important to remember to be positive.

Without this positivity, you will find that it is hard to keep going. It is easy to become really overwhelmed with all of the things that come with this branding. And if you allow yourself to get down with it, and not keep up the positivity, then it is hard for you to get it all done.

If you are worried about keeping up with your positivity, then start each day with the positivity that you need. You can start out with some good affirmations. You can choose to listen to some upbeat music. You can remind yourself of how it is going to feel when you finally reach your goals!

Be dedicated

Working on your own personal brand is not something that you can do part time. It isn't something that you can bring out when you have some free time, and hope that it is all going to work out for you. It isn't something that is always easy. Instead, you need to be able to dedicate your time to making this all happen. Creating your own personal brand takes time, and you need to be wiling to constantly work on updating it, improving it, and more.

If you are not able to spend at least a bit of time each day on making this personal brand, and you aren't willing to work hard to see the results, then you may as well stop now. Those who see the success that you are working for with this kind of branding, are the ones who understood how much dedication it takes.

The good news is, if you are passionate about your brand, and you are ready to make this personal brand grow your fortune and get you the fame that you want, this kind of dedication isn't going to be too hard. You may need to come up with a schedule to remind yourself of what to get done. This can help you to stay on track, even if you are busy with other things, like children, work, and school, you will still get the work done when it needs to get done.

Be passionate

Don't just put out some content just because you think it will get others to look at you. You need to be able to show passion to others about whatever you are showing off. Your personal brand can't just be some words on a page. Remember, there are a ton of other people who are trying to do the same thing that you are doing. And unless you want to be like most of them and you want to end up disappearing into nothing soon after you start, then you need to make sure that you are able to really make yourself stand out with something special.

Having a passion for your brand, even if it is a personal brand, and being able to show that passion in all of the stuff that you release to the public, will make a difference. Your consumer is smart. They know when you are actually passionate about something, or when you are just trying to put things up and trying to make money from them. Make sure that your passion is showing through; otherwise, it may be time to reconsider what you are doing since it won't bring you the passion that you want.

Be focused

When you are working on your own personal brand, you need to learn how to be focused. If you only work on the process every once in a while, if you spend too much time putting up random stuff that doesn't go together, and if you mess around and don't take all of this as seriously as it deserves, then you are going to run into trouble.

There are a lot of people out there who are trying to work with their own personal branding. This means that there is a lot of competition and noise out there. you need to be able to stand out from the crowd. And if you, and your campaign, doesn't have focus, this is something that will never happen. Learning how to focus your energy, and to keep your campaign working well can be the key that you need to help you to stand out and get others to notice you.

Be open to input

As you create your own personal brand, you will have a lot of learning to do. You won't know it all, and you may need the help of others to make sure that you are prepared and ready to take your brand to the next level. If you refuse to listen to any of the input that others give to you, then there is no way that you are going to be able to improve your brand, and you are more likely to fail.

This can be hard to do. There are always plenty of people who are willing to provide you with advice, and most of them have never done anything like this in the past, so they have no experience to help you. You have to be able to sort through all the noise and find the advice that is actually going to work for you, and not listen to everyone. This doesn't mean that you should avoid all advice and input though.

When you start posting about yourself online, and you work on your personal brand on places like YouTube, Instagram, Facebook, and more, you may find that everyone has an opinion. And most of these are not going to be the nicest. Many people have opinions about everything, even if they have no experience, and since they can hide behind a computer screen, they aren't afraid of sharing their opinion. This is probably not where you should get your advice from. Even if there are some good points hidden in the comments somewhere, it is likely that you are going to read a ton of negative, and not helpful, comments before that.

If you can, look for a mentor instead. Find someone who has worked on personal branding in the past, and then ask for their input. They may have some criticisms for you along the way as well. But at least this will be done as a way to make you more successful, not just a way to be mean. If you can find those who will be able to help you to promote your brand, and get the right persona out to others.

Have a purpose for all you do

When you are working on your personal brand, you need to make sure that everything has a purpose. You want it all to work well together. You don't want to go way off the path and turn others off from what you are doing with the rest of your work. You can't try things that are out of the norm, or things that don't' have a purpose, or you are going to turn others away from what you are doing.

This means that you will need to take some time to really think through all of the things that you post and put out there for others to see. It is fine to experiment a little and see if something works. But you need to think about everything that you are doing before you decide to let it out there. if it isn't going to work for promoting yourself, then it is time for you to make some changes.

When you are ready to work on your own personal brand, you need to make sure that you are in the right mentality. While there are a lot of different things that you are able to do to promote your own personal brand, you have to remember that there is going to be a lot of things that can go wrong. And with all of the people online, you will find that there are always people who will want to bring you down, who won't like what you are doing, and can say mean things along the way. Having the right mentality, and the right plan, from the beginning an make a big difference in the amount of success that you are going to see.

Chapter 3: What is Needed to Build Your Own Personal Brand

Now that we understand a bit more about this personal branding and what it is all about, it is time to build up the foundation for your own personal brand. This foundational work is going to eb something that you need to build up as time goes on, and in the long run, making changes and working hard on this personal brand will make a big difference in what you are able to do.

If you ever want to go on a career where you want to see success in the public eye, or one that is going to need you to have a good reputation with others, then finding a way to make your own personal brand is so important. Basically, personal branding is going to be essential for most professionals, although it is rarely used. The good news with this is that, since so few other people are doing this right now, you will have the upper hand.

Since this personal branding can be so important when it comes to what you can see with your personal success. Some of the things that you need in order to start building up your own brand will include:

Technology

Technology rules the world, and having a few basic components of technology can make a difference when you are creating your personal brand. First, you need to have a phone with you. And since you will need to be able to take calls, look up information, take pictures, download information to your social media sites, do live videos and more, it is probably best to aim for a smartphone. If you decide to keep a tablet on hand and use this for that purpose, then you may be able to get away with a simple phone, but most entrepreneurs like yourself will want the smartphone.

When picking out the smartphone, consider a few things. Look at how many pictures you can take on it, how sturdy it is (you will be taking it around with you on a regular basis so you want it to be able to stand the test of time). You can also look for a nice warranty to help you keep it in good shape as you move around.

Having some kind of computer will help as well. A laptop is a nice addition because it allows you to move around and do your work from where is the most convenient for you, but some people find that they prefer a desktop computer. Pick out the option that works the best for you. As you work on your personal brand, you are going to spend some time on this device, so going with one that is in good shape, and that has the right programming will make a big difference in the success that you gain.

Depending on the kind of thing that you are going to focus on with this endeavor, you may find that there are other options that you may need. Having a tablet is a must for some personal branders, as well as a good camera, good video camera, and more. Consider what you will need in order to get started and make sure you have the best to make this work better for you.

Knowledge about your topic of interest

No matter what industry you are trying to get into, you need to have a lot of knowledge to help you get started. there is a lot of competition out there for the consumer, and if you aren't knowledgeable about what you an bring to the table, then they will go with someone else.

Let's say that you are looking to get a job in the computer technology field. Would it make much sense for someone to hire you if you couldn't list off some of the basic programs that you can work with? Would they be likely to hire you if you weren't able to talk about computers, technology, and other similar topics? As someone who is trying to get the job, and why may be competing against a lot of other people who have more experience, you really need to sell yourself. And one way to do this is to know about the topic.

If you are able to come into that interview and talk about the topic, talk about some of the newest innovations with that topic, and get into a good conversation about it with the person interviewing you, it is more likely that they will take an interest. And if they are able to visit your social media sites, your own website if you have one, and look at your resume and cover letter and they all match up in showing your knowledge and interest about the topic, and shows your personal brand well, then you are more likely to get the job.

This can be true if you are trying to build up your own persona online as well. If you are trying to do a YouTube channel about building cars, you need to make sure that you are the best out there at making cars. You have to convince the consumer that you really know what you are talking about, that you are confident in your skills, and that it is worth their time to watch you, rather than someone else.

A good mindset

You talked about the idea of a good mindset earlier. If you start out on this process feeling down about yourself, or that it is not going to work out for you, then you will fail. But if you can come in with some positivity, with the determination and dedication to keep on moving, and some good goals in place, then you have the right mindset to make sure that you will be successful with this endeavor in no time.

Good social skills

It is impossible to make a good personal brand if you don't have the right social skills in place. Without these social skills, it is hard for you to meet new people, and form the connections that you need to see some results. Any time that you are building up a personal brand, and when you are trying to get that job, increase your reach on social media, or do any of your other goals, you are going to need to be able to build up some good social skills in the process.

There are a lot of things that you can work on when it comes to your social skills. Even if you feel shy or like you are not good with talking to others, this is something important to work on because it will ensure that you are able to reach your target market. To start with this, work on your eye contact. You will form a good connection with the other person if you are able to look them in the eyes when you are talking to them. This shows that you are truly interested in what they are telling you. If this seems awkward, look at their nose or just right below the eyes.

You can also mimic the other person a bit. This isn't meant for you to copy them and make fun of them. But make sure to watch how they hold themselves, how they move their hands, how they are standing, and how they talk. If you are then able to subtly follow these cues, you will get them to feel more at ease with you.

If you find that it is hard to get a good conversation started with the other person, then it is a good idea for you to come prepared with a few topics to get you going. This isn't meant for you to get stuck on a script. That will sound awkward and can make it difficult and stops the conversation in no time. Using these as guides, and then letting the conversation flow, can make a big difference though.

And finally, just go for it. Yes, it can be hard to network and talk to others. And yes there are times when you and the other person may not click and you don't get the response that is needed. But it is still important to get out there and make sure that you form some kind of connection with as many people as possible. Without good social skills, you will not be able to network and share information about your brand. Get out there, meet some new people, and remember that it is so important to socialize to increase your brand awareness.

Chapter 4: The Steps You Need to Begin Your Personal Brand

Now it is time to look at some of the steps that you need in order to ep build up that personal brand. Building this kind of brand can take some time. it isn't something that will happen to you overnight, and it definitely will not happen without some work ahead of time. but for those who are willing to put in the time, and give it their all, it can be a great thing, and will progress you in so many ways. When you are ready to learn more about creating your own personal brand, make sure to check out this guidebook to help you get started.

Identify what you have to offer others

No matter who you are, you are going to have some qualities that will make you unique. There is something that is special inside all of us, something that will make it so that others want to get to know us. Maybe it is your sense of humor, a winning smile. Maybe you are able to take a look at a situation and give some good advice to someone else. The positive aspects that come with your personality are going to be things that you need to focus on going forward when it comes to the personal brand you want to create. After all, personal branding has been described as selling the idea of a relationship with you to other people. With this in mind, you want to strive to sell the other people the best experience of you possible.

If you find that it is difficult to identify the best qualities that you can offer to other people, then it is time to enlist some help. You can talk to some family or friends, people who are looking to help you and who know you the best. Take a sampling of a few different people, ones who aren't too biased will be the best, in order to help you to figure out what unique personality traits and hobbies that you can bring to the table.

Remember, these good qualities don't have to just be things about your personality. You could include a lot of good things about yourself, no matter what area of your life they tend to come from. Everything has the some kind of value in what you bring to the table any time that you decide to make your own personal brand.

For example, maybe you are really good at color combination and wardrobe styling. Maybe you are good with programming and other things of technology. These are known as ancillary attributes. They won't be the main trait that you are trying to package into this personal brand, and they will not be the trade that you choose to capitalize on. However, these are less pronounced and smaller skills that are still really important and will be able to help you out along the way.

With this you will be able to come up wit your own little profile of yourself, one that you are able to use in order to further your brand. We are going to take a look at one of these as an example. Remember that you are allowed to write down as much as you would like, but in the end, you will need to come up with just one that you would like to focus on. It is great if you are able to make a nice list of all of these to showcase your strengths and your hobbies, but this can cause you to balance too many plates at once, and can make it hard for the consumer to follow you. Narrowing it down a bit can make a big difference. Some of the things that you may write down about yourself (but you can only choose one in each category) includes:

Personally traits:

1. Maybe a personality trait is going to be funny. You notice that you are able to make a lot of the people around you laugh on a regular basis, and it make you feel good that you can make other people laugh.
2. Informed. This could be a trait if you are someone who is always researching the current events around them, and trying to figure out which side of the argument is the best.

3. Creative: You may see this one as a personality trait because you are able to see things in multiple different ways. You may be able to turn nothing into something, in a way that others just can't manage to do.

Ancillary skills:

1. Good with speaking in speaking.
2. Crafty. You like to build things, and you like to spend your time working on something new.
3. Technology.

With these things in mind, it is possible that you can come up with a few possibilities for how you are able to sell yourself, and this can make up your own personal brand. Maybe you would be able to teach, creating a variety of videos, books, and blogs about a topic. Maybe you could become a public voice or do some kind of talking, like a podcast. Along with the crafty part, you could use crafts and sell them on platforms and make money in that manner as well.

Once you have been able to go through and come up with your profile qualities, it is time to move on to the next step and research some of the options that you have for personal branding.

Research the types of personal brands, and then pick one out.

There are going to be different types of personal branding that you are able to pick out. And the one that you choose to go with is going to depend on the specific goals that you are looking to achieve. The most common form, and the one that is the easiest to work with, is going to be known as interpersonal branding.

When you are working with interpersonal branding, you are going to curate a persona, along with social media accounts, for the people in your personal life, such as your family and your friends. While this may sound a little bit deceptive, it is just a bit more concentrated effort to do what we have been taught to do since we were born. We do not say certain things to others because of how it may make us look, we do not flaunt or open up about our flaws until we get to know others well.

Basically, you will find that interpersonal branding is just going to take those natural tendencies that we have one step further and giving our social lives more attention. This may mean that you go through the social media accounts that you have, and polishing them up a bit. You can choose to give them a theme that is cohesive, and make them look more professional.

The next kind of personal branding that you can work with is going to be known as professional persona branding. This is going to be a branding type where a person wishes to take their professional set of skills, and then self-package it along with their professional skills so that they can seem more desirable to current and potential employers.

When you decide that it is time to create your own professional personal brand, you would either change your personal social media sites, or create a new one, and add in some more professional content compared to what you would have done in the past.

When you are working with this kind of branding, you have to pay attention to who would actually come to the social media platform to look at you. If you are trying to further your own career, or you are interested in impressing some of the people who are calling you for interviews in your own industry, then the professional personal branding is the right option for you. But you need to make sure that the information they see, the information that they are in contact with, will need to be professional, on target, and not include any gossip or other issues in the way.

Then you can move to the highest level of personal branding. This is what a lot of people are going to think about when they ear the term personal branding. The other two options that we talked about before will fall under this as well.

Personal branding, when we look at it in its fullest form, is when you are going to package together your skills set, social accounts, aesthetic, name, face, and personality and then you market it towards the public eye. This one is going to take some time and a lot of effort, but, if you are able to do it in a successful manner, you will be able to get the most benefits.

Many people who decide to turn their whole lives around and make that into a brand are the ones who would like to be in the public eye. This can be online or through some of the other media outlets that are available. And to be successful with this, you need to be willing to create a lot of content that is entertaining, creative and innovative, especially since you are competing with others who want the same goas, and you are trying to make yourself stand out.

So, from here you need to take some time and figure out which of the persona branding types you would like to work with. Do you want to just be socially seen in one way or another? Do you want to make sure that you are going to impress a current or potential employer wit your information? Or would you like to change up everything, and make your own persona for others to find online, and so that you can figure out new ways to create your own wealth.

Set your goals

Never start on your own personal brand without having some goals in mind. It may seem like a great idea to just run in head first and see what happens, but everyone who has tried to do that has failed in the long run. You have a lot of competition out there, and if you go in without any goals, and no idea on how far you should be, and at what point, it is going to be almost impossible for you to see the results that you want.

Before you get too far into this process, sit back and consider where you would like to go. What would success look like for you? Write that down, and then see if you are able to break it down into some smaller pieces. Working just towards one big goal, without separating it out into some little goals, can create a big mess. You will get worn out before long, and not feel like you accomplished anything in the process.

After you break down the little goals, you can start writing out a schedule of when you would like these to be done. Be reasonable here. You don't want to set the deadline for so far in the future that there is no motivation for you to work hard and get them done. But you also don't want to set them so close that there is no chance. Maybe set the first few goals and see how that goes, and then adjust the rest of the goals from there.

As you accomplish each goal, you will be able to celebrate a little bit. It is a big accomplishment just working on your own personal branding, and it is something that can take some time and effort in order to accomplish. you should stop and take some time to celebrate all of the hard work that you have put in so far each time you reach a new goal.

Figure out who your audience will be

The next thing that you need to consider when you are trying to get started with your own personal brand is trying to figure out who the target audience will be. You are not going to be able to reach everyone with all of your message. There are just too many people out there, and this can waste a lot of time, money, and talents. Figuring out who your audience members will be can make a world of difference.

For example, if you are trying to make yourself into a YouTube star, your personal brand would look a bit different compared to someone who just left college and is trying to entice some of the employers that they applied with to look at their information. You would not want to waste your time and set up the same kind of campaign to handle bot of these.

Knowing your audience is going to make the process of personal branding so much easier than before. It will help you to know what kind of content you should write, what should be in the content, and even the different media sources that you should use. Make sure that right from the beginning you sit down and come up with the perfect target audience. This doesn't have to be difficult. Just think about who you would like to see this information once you are done with it.

You may find that you need to write this information out a bit before you get started. You can write out the words about the kind of personality or audience that you would like to work with. Or you can consider trying to write out a story about this person and some of their likes or dislikes are. You can keep this near you. It will ensure that you are able to keep your information on target, and that all of the parts of the campaign will stick together.

Find your team

Now one is able to create this kind of personal brand all on their own, no matter how much they may wish so. You are going to need a team of people who are able to support and to guide you trough all of this process. Those who will help you emotionally as you get started with this could include people from your family, or your friends. You could find a team who will help you gain the necessary resources, and who are able to invest with their time or financially to ensure that you are able to launch your brand.

There are a lot of different things that can go on when you are trying to create your own personal brand. Doing it alone just adds in a lot of extra work that you are not really supposed to handle on your own. Having people who can support you emotionally and financially, and having those who can bounce your ideas from and answer your questions, will ensure that your new brand can get off the ground.

Gather the resources that you need

The resources that we are talking about here will include anything that you are able to use in order to further your brand, and to help you reach your goals. The common thoughts on this right now includes three main types of resources, including treasure, talent and your time.

Your time is going to be any tie that you and your team will have in investing in your new personal brand. In order to figure out the type of time investment that you are able to make (because no one is able to work on this nonstop 24/7, you need to look at your current lifestyle and how much time you are able to give to this, and the availability of your team members as well.

If you are currently working a job that is from 9 to 5 each day, and you still plan to launch a personal brand, then you may find that more treasure or talent will be needed to make this a reality, because you may not be able to invest as time into it. And since you already went through and took stock of this resource before the process, you should have a pretty good idea of how much time you can invest into the whole process.

And when you decide to evaluate the treasure, you need to include material possessions along with your money. Things like the technology that you took the time to invest in, the software that you purchased, and even the clothes that you will wear can all come in and contribute to your personal brand.

Remember that investing your own wealth can add to the risk, and it certainly is riskier than investing your talent or your time. if you fail with tis process because you did not put in the work, it is possible to walk away form all of this with the talent in hand. And you are provided with some more time each day of the week. But your wealth is an investment that you are not able to get back ever. So, if you are going to invest a lot of money into this process, take the time to make sure that you are investing that money in the right way, in the manner that will make you feel comfortable and won't be adding in more risk than is necessary.

Begin to pour the foundation

When you have gotten this far, you should have been able to identify the thing that you are able to offer to the world. You will have a good idea of the type of personal branding that you would like to pursue, and you should have gone through and set up some new goals for yourself to help you get there. and this is just the start!

Once you are here, it is time for you to start the tangible work of creating your own personal brand. This means that you will need to go in and do the actual work of hanging your social media accounts, dressing in the wardrobe that you chose, creating content for your target audience, and basically just doing the steps that we talked about above for your own personal branding.

The steps that you do here are going to vary based on your overall goals with this personal branding, and what you would ike to see happen. Maybe you will spend some time taking pictures and videos that you are able to upload. You may go through and upload a few pictures to YouTube to showcase your products or some of your message. You may take any step that is necessary in order to get that new persona up and running, which can make it easier to sell it across all of the different platforms that you want.

Creating your own personal brand is something that can take some time, and some effort. It is not always as easy as it may seem, and lots of people have spent a lot of time trying to do for themselves. Creating a personal brand, whether you are doing it for personal reasons, professional reasons, and even for becoming more popular and like a celebrity, you will find that these steps will help you to get started in no time!

Chapter 5: Remember to Be Yourself

When you are working on your own personal brand, you will want to make sure that you are always yourself. It is sometimes hard to at like yourself when you start to post online. You may be worried about what others think about you. You may want to come off as cooler, or funnier, or something else when you work on this personal branding.

When you are trying to make up your new persona, and you are trying to get other consumers to like you, it is easy to try too hard sometimes. Or you may find that you see some negative comments come up on your page and you then decide to change up everything about yourself in order to try to change the opinions and make sure that you are more likeable to others.

However, even when you are trying to create your own persona, you need to make sure that you are still acting like yourself. This is one of the best ways to impress those who are watching your content, and will ensure that you are able to get the best results with your personal brand. People can see right through something that is fake, so don't waste your time, or their time either.

Since you are creating your own personal brand it is sometimes hard to remember that you can be yourself. But if you want to avoid the risk of turning others away from you and losing your target audience, then this is one of the most important things that you are able to do for your business. Let's take a look at a few of the things that you are able to do to ensure that you can be yourself, even when you are working on a personal brand.

Make your own hobbies a part of your brand

Whether you have a love for a certain sports team, you like to read, you like to fish, or your interest is less common, you can definitely use your hobbies in your personal brand. In fact, adding these in and talking about them, at least on occasion, is a great way to add some new life to your brand, and will ensure that it can stand out from the crowd.

Adding in these hobbies and interest will go a long way when it comes to making you more interesting and more genuine. And this is a great way for you to find a way to bond with your prospects and your clients who have interests that are similar to yours.

Show off the family

You don't need to show off every detail about your family to make this one happen. But if you are married and you have kids, or even if you are just married, then they are going to be a big part of your life. You should consider making them a part of your personal brand. You can do this by adding pictures of them on your social media accounts, and talking about them. There are a lot of ways to do this naturally, and it can really make a difference in the amount of connection that you can form with those around you.

Don't be shy

Even if you are a shy person in real life, it is important that you take the time to be a bit more outgoing when promoting your own personal brand. You need to really show others your true self so that they can start to know you and want to follow you. Even someone who is shy has a lot of other aspects about them. You just need to be willing to jump over that hurdle of being shy and make sure that you are showing these sides.

You will find that it is much easier to be engaging and interesting when you get over the hurdle of being shy. Even those who are really shy have something of value that they are able to give to those around them. This is a great thing to get you out of your shell as well. You have no chance of getting the results that you want and building up a personal brand, if you still stay shy.

The good news is that it is possible for you to be more outgoing, without even needing to talk to anyone else. A lot of the ways that we can build up a business in this modern world is online. If you do a YouTube video, you may have to get out of your shell a bit more to really impress the consumer because they are seeing you face to face. But

PERSONAL BRANDING

if you write a blog, or try to promote things on your social media account, you will be able to reach out to that potential customer through the words you write, rather than talking to them in person. This alone should make it so much easier for even the shy person to step in and see some results.

No matter what though, you need to make sure that your real personality has some room to come out and shine. You do not want to end up with a lot of people turning away because you hide things, or you are too nervous to actually talk about what you want.

Act like your consumers are your best friends

When you are posting anything online, such as on social media, when you make a YouTube video, or when you write in your blog, one way to make sure that you are really showing off your good side, and your true self, is to pretend that the reader is your best friend. Pretend that you have known them for years, and that you both share a lot of secrets and fun times and laughter together through the years.

When you put a face to the audience, and you see them as friends, it is easier to be open and honest with them. It takes away some of the nerves that you are feeling, and makes it easier to work with them, to tell them more about you, and to drop the act of being fake and trying to impress them.

If it helps, write out a description of who you are talking to when you do this process. You can write a little backstory about them, their name, what they look like, and how you would like to talk with them. You can even put up a picture of one of your current best friends and pretend that you are writing the posts and01 the blogs and more in order to make it easier when you write.

Don't be fake

There are countless social media accounts out there that include people who just aren't able to be themselves. You take a look at them, and after just a few posts, or a few pictures, you know that they are just fake and full of themselves. These people have the perfect hair all the time, the perfect bodies, perfect families, and perfect life. You read through the information, and there is never one complaint to worry about at all.

While it is always a good thing to count our blessings and to be thankful for what we have, even when there may be some bad things going on, it is important to note that you shouldn't come off as fake. There is something as too perfect, even when you are on social media, and your audience is going to be able to spot this from a mile away. You have probably gone through a few of these profiles and thought how there is nothing substantial there, and that this person isn't really sharing the real them at all. This is a big turn off to many people in your audience.

Sure, you don't need to spend all of your time bashing those in your life and complaining that nothing seems to go your way. this is going to backfire against you as well and can turn a lot of your audience away. There needs to be a good balance here. Showing some of your vulnerabilities, like how you are human too, and how you do go through some struggles at the same time as well, can make a big difference in how people respond to you.

This again goes back to the marketing plan that you come up with for your brand. How do you want people to perceive you, and what kinds of posts are you going to put up in order to help you to accomplish this? If you decide to plan out some of your posts ahead of time, then you will be able to plan it out so you can have some real life posts, some humorous ones, some that are going to be informative, and some where you show the good things in your life.

Try to keep the drama at home

While you are supposed to spend some time working on showing your true self, you do need to filter it at least a little bit. You do not need to tell your consumer every little thing about yourself. There are some things that you want to leave at home. And this includes all of the drama, and much of the bad stuff.

When you are showing little parts about your personal life, remember that it needs to match up to the brand that you are trying to create. If it doesn't, then there is no reason to bring it out. Talking about a fight that you just got done having with your spouse is just going to seem petty and mean. And it is going to turn a lot of people off from you, especially if it just happened and the emotions are raw, and you are mad.

However, there is a way that you can use this to your advantage. Maybe you write a blog about parenting or relationships. While you don't want to go on social media and blast your partner right after the fight, you could take the lessens that you learn from that fight, and maybe write a blog about it. You can add in the personal details a bit (but not so much that it looks like you are just trying to get attention), to help prove your point or show the readers how you were able to get trough it. Of course, if you are working on a finance blog or a cooking blog or something that has nothing to do with the fight that you and your spouse just had, then eave that drama at home.

The image that you give out to others is important. Everything that you showcase on your blog, your social media accounts, and more, needs to match up with the brand that you are trying to sell. If it doesn't, then leave that information at home. But, no matter what kind of personal brand you are trying to create, you may find that adding in a personal touch, and showing your audience the real you will make a world of difference. It makes you seem more in touch with them, shows them something that is unique, and can make it easier for them to connect to you. Just make sure that you pick out stories, interests, and other things to share that are going to progress your brand, not ones that are going to put you in a bad light and turns others away from you.

Chapter 6: How to Choose Your Audience

Before you get too into making your personal brand, you need to take some time to really know your audience. It is impossible to market yourself to everyone. It would be nice if we were able to do that, but everyone throughout the whole country, no matter what the age, gender, job type and more, are not all going to like the same things. Know who will enjoy your information the most, and then putting your marketing efforts towards that will make a big difference in how well you turn your material to fit them, and how much money you can actually make with this.

Think of it this way. Person A is going to start a blog about parenting. They will most likely want to look for an audience who is about to have children, or who already have children, and who would like to have some advice about things that they are dealing with. They will look for mostly moms, and maybe some dads, with younger children. And they may choose to go with people who are a certain age, and in a certain location as well.

Then we move to Person B. This person is looking to get a job in accounting and wants to make a personal brand based on getting this job. They are not likely to want the same audience as what Person A wants because stay at home mothers are not going to hire them for an accounting job. They are going to look for employers who will hire them and will make that their target audience.

So, because there are so many different people throughout the world, and they all have different needs that should be met, you need to be able to come up with your own target audience to ensure that you can reach them, and that you provide them with information and content that they want.

This is going to vary depending on the audience that you want to reach and the topic that you want to focus your branding on. But no matter what your personal brand is about, there are a few things that you can consider when you are trying to pick out your target audience. These things will include:

1. What age they are. Usually this is going to be an age range, rather than an exact age that you will use. For example, you may decide that your target age range is going to be 25 to 35.
2. Gender: In some cases, you may find that you will go with male and female, but then other times, you may just want to go with one gender over the other. Decide which one works the best for what you want to accomplish.
3. Do they have a family? Does your target audience have a spouse, children, or other family members that are important to them?
4. Where do they work. The profession that the target audience has is going to influence their thoughts, hobbies and more so this is something that you should consider before you move forward.
5. What do they like to do in their free time understanding the hobbies of your target can help you determine if they are interested in what you are writing about. You should consider if you are able to make content that goes towards this or not.
6. Where they live. Knowing where the target audience lives is going to make a big difference as well. People are often going to respond in different ways based on where they live and what they are accustomed to.

These are just a few of the things that you need to consider when you are picking out your personal branding technique. There are a lot of different aspects that you can consider, based on the topic and theme that you are basing your personal brand on. Make sure that you are working to create a cohesive look to your personal brand so you can get the best results here.

One good activity that you can do here to make it easier to pick out your target audience is to write out what you imagine the perfect target audience member will be. Think about who they are, if they are male or female, what they look like, how old they are, what they do for a job, the things that they like to do for fun, whether they have a family, if they like to travel for work, and more. Write down a backstory to go with the target audience as well if you find that this is the best way to get that person stuck in your head.

Once this is done, you will need to keep this paper around. Place it somewhere that you will be able to get to easily any time that you write out a blog post, or you post in social media, or do anything else with your brand. Think about whether this message will speak to your target audience or not. Think abut what would impress them, and what they would like to hear. Then, use that to help direct your messages so that you stay on track, and you really work to build up your personal brand.

Chapter 7: The Importance of Having a Mentor

Another thing that you should consider when you get started with having your own personal brand is a mentor. Going it alone, especially with all of the competition that is out there and all of the noise that you have to fight against, can make this even more challenging. If you are able to find a mentor to work with you on all of this, someone who is going to guide you, give you advice, tell you when something is working and when it doesn't, and point you in the right direction, will give you a leg up on the competition and will ensure that you will actually be successful when you start your persona brand.

So, how do you go about finding the mentor you would like to work with? Look in your industry. You want to be able, if you can, find someone who has experience with personal branding in your own industry or your own niche. These individuals will have the specific experience that you are looking for, which makes them a goldmine of information to help you. They can walk you trough the exact process that they did, and if you do it the right way, you will be able to see the success as well.

Of course, you may not be able to find someone who is in your niche. This is especially true if you are working on a new niche or one that hasn't been done very much. Or maybe you just can't find someone who is interested. There are still other places you can look in order to find the mentor you would like to work with.

You may find that talking to someone who has done personal branding in a completely different niche. Or even talking with someone who has done branding for another business before. This may not give you quite the same insights as you would find when you are working with a mentor in your own niche, but it can make a big difference.

They can still offer you a lot of the advice and tips on how to make your strategy better than ever.

At this point, you may want to figure out how to get someone to agree to be your mentor. First, you need to ask them. If you don't ask someone to be your mentor, how are they going to know that you need their help? You may be surprised at how many people, once you flatter them a bit, and explain that you think they are successful enough that you want them to be your mentor, will be more than happy to step up and help you out.

Using a bit of flattery in here can help as well. And showing them how it will benefit them, rather than just having all of the benefits go straight to you, will make a difference as well. Remember, these people have spent a lot of time working with their own personal brand up to this point, and they need to keep working hard to maintain it. They need to be able to see the benefit of doing this as well.

Some of these mentors will be happy to help out someone else because of the flattery, and because of you just asking. But if you are able to sweeten the pot a bit, and offer them something in exchange for their time, then that is a good thing to work on as well. You can consider giving them some recognition on your bog, mention them to your followers, once you get those built up a bit. Get creative here. Depending on who you decide to work with, there could be quite a few others who are talking to this person as well, and you want to be able to offer something that is different and unique.

Once you have been able to get the mentor to agree to work with you for some time, it is important that you don't waste their time. they are busy as well, and you don't want to end up with spending hours with them and not getting anything done. Before you meet up with them for the first time, after they have agreed to help you in the role of a mentor, you should take the time to write down the questions that you have. bring some examples of your blog posts, or your social media posts, and show them what you plan to do.

The more prepared that you can be for this meeting, the better it is for the both of you. When you have all of this information together and ready to go, you will find that it is easier for the mentor to provide you with advice, suggestions, and answers along the way. if you show up with nothing prepared, you just won't get as much out of the meeting as you really could.

If you are able to, try to set up the mentor relationship so that you can meet with them more than one time. there are a lot of things that are going to grow and develop with your personal brand over the years. Just getting advice at the beginning, and never double checking later on, will make it hard for you to grow over time. It is much better for you to spend your time meeting up with the mentor on occasion, even if it is just every few months, or a few times a year.

This is a hard thing to do sometimes. You and your mentor are often going to be busy, and finding times to do this together can be hard. But if you are prepared to work on your personal brand, and you want to be able to really make sure that you can get ahead, then this is something that you need to make important in your life and make sure that you are able to get the most out of these meetings.

During this time, remember that your mentor may not always tell you what you want to hear. There are times when they are going to talk to you, and tell you that you are doing something wrong, or that you need to go trough and change things up. Don't take this in a personal way. You wanted the mentor to make sure that you are able to get the most out of your personal brand. This means that if you do something wrong, you want to make sure that you get it fixed as soon as possible.

Yes, you may have worked hard on something for a long period of time, and are proud of the work that you did. And yes, it may mean that you will need to redo the work on occasion. But isn't it much better to hear about the stuff that you are doing wrong now, before you let it go on too long and drive away the customers and your personal branding goes out the window.

Having a mentor can be one of the best things that you can do when you are working on your personal brand. They will be able to tell you what is working, and what isn't working, so that you can do the best for your personal brand.

Chapter 8: Why Do I Need a Good Team to Help Me Get Started

If you are just working on making a personal brand in order to get that job that you have had your eye on for some time, then you will probably be able to do all of this branding on your own. You are just trying to gain a good reputation amongst a small market, and you will find that your employer will see you if you put in some time.

But if you are trying to grow a personal brand in order to sell something, or to promote yourself in a blog, videos, or some other way, then it is likely that you will need to reach a much bigger audience than you would have had to do in the past. Because of this, it is likely that you will need to take some time to find a good team to help you get started.

There is a lot of work that is going to go into turning that personal branding into something that is successful. It takes some time, and many times you are not able to do all of the work on your own. Working with a team, even if it ends up being just one or two people, will make a difference in how successful you are in the future. Some of the people that you should consider adding to your team will include:

Camera crew

The camera crew is going to be something to consider if you would like to create some high-quality videos. Remember that on YouTube, there are a lot of videos already present there. if you are building up your personal brand, you won't stand a chance if your videos look bad, the listener is not able to hear you, or there is something else that is low-quality about the video.

If you are just posting a few quick videos on some of the other social media sites that you are on, then you can probably do them yourself and your smartphone may be just fine. But many people find that a great way to build up the personal brand that they have is to work on some short video series on YouTube, and other platforms.

For those who are going with this second option, you need to find a way to stand out form the crowd. And having some high-quality videos, ones that are professionally done, will help you brand get the recognition that it needs, much faster than anything else. And it is unlikely that you will be able to do this all on your own.

Hiring at least one person, and maybe a crew, of people who know how to work with this kind of thing, and who will be able to walk you trough it all, capture the videos, do the editing, and upload it all in a professional manner, will make a big difference in the amount of success that you are likely to see. Don't believe that this is true? Try doing one video that is higher quality, and one that is lower quality and see how the views are different. Or find a low quality video on YouTube and monitor your own reaction to it.

Wardrobe

If you plan on doing a lot of videos on YouTube, then you may find that hiring someone to help you wit your wardrobe will make a big difference. This may seem like a silly thing to work on, but it is going to take a big difference in how well you are going to do. People, hopefully a lot of them, are going to see your videos, and you want to make sure that you come across as professional, and looking good in the process.

This one is not as important if you are working with other forms of promoting your personal brand. But if you plan to do a lot of pictures or a lot of videos, it may be worth your time to talk to someone about your style choices, and have someone, even if it is a friend who is good at designing or style, come in and discuss it with you. You want to make sure that you are really impressing the people who are going to watch your videos, and the outfits you wear, as well as the information you present and the way you present it, will make a difference in how they perceive you.

Marketing

At some point, you will hopefully be able to get your personal brand up and running to a point where you will see some tremendous results. But even in the beginning, you may find that a little bit of marketing can go a long way. marketing will ensure that you are able to reach the right target audience, no matter where they are, and it ensures that your message will get right out there to them.

Marketing can be hard to do, especially for those who are not really well-versed in making it happen. If you have never done this marketing in the past, and if you aren't sure about the first place to start, then it may be a good idea to have someone who does know about this take control for you. This can ensure that you will be able to reach the right people, at the right time.

The nice thing about having a person who is good at marketing, and who has done this in the past, is they can take all of the individual parts you have been working on, and bring them altogether. If you have a Facebook account, a blog, and Instagram account, and some videos on YouTube, then a good marketer is able to put together all of these parts, and ensure that they are cohesive, and that they can work together to make each one more powerful.

You can certainly try to do some of this on your own if you want. And it may be able to save you some money in the process as well. But this takes time, and learning the marketing system of each individual part of the process (such as how to do Facebook marketing and Instagram marketing) can take a lot of time. Having a professional will make a big difference.

Social media

Many times, as you are building your personal brand, you will find that it is going to be a smaller endeavor. Many of those who are trying to build up a personal brand are going to start out basically. If you are just making a personal brand so that you become more employable in an industry, it is likely that you just have a few social media sites running, and you are keeping it all on a small scale. But if you want to take it to the next level and have a big personal brand, like what we see with the celebrities and some other well-known people, then you are going to need to bump up your social media presence.

When you start, it is your job to maintain the social media accounts. And it is probably a good idea for you to be the one to maintain them for as long as possible. You can consider having a team around who will be able to advice you of the best way to keep that account going, when to post, and to look over the analytics with you.

But these social media accounts are meant to be your own personal voice. You are supposed to show more about your products, share information that you think that others in your target audience are going to enjoy, and really showcase your own hobbies, interests, and more on there as well. This needs to be a nice personal touch. You can have your team do all that they want with the other parts of your brand, but for the most part, your target audience still expects that you are going to be the one who runs your own social media accounts.

The second that you start letting someone else do this, it is going to cause some issues with your brand. You will start to lose some of your own voice. You may find that the other person, even if they have a lot of experience behind them, just doesn't get the voice that you are trying to portray here. And you may find that you are going to miss the mark with your consumer.

Since social media is going to be a huge way that you meet up with and interact with your target audience, this is not a place that you want to leave to chance or have mess up for you. Doing the work on your own, even if you have to go through and make some of the posts on your own ahead of time and schedule them for yourself, can make a big difference in the interaction and the connection that you will make with your consumer.

Strategy planning

In the beginning, you are going to be the one who needs to get in there and create the winning strategy that you will use. You need to have an idea about the social media sites that you will post on, the target audience you would like to work with, and all of the other factors that you are going to work with. In the beginning, it is likely that you will keep it pretty small, working with just one or two social media accounts, and maybe a blog to make this easier to manage.

Hopefully, if you are successful, your brand is going to start growing. And as you see it grow, the strategy is going to be much harder for you to manage on your own. This is when you may want to consider working with a strategy planning team. They will have a lot more resources than you to figure out what is working on your brand, and what you may need to change.

This doesn't mean that you need to completely get yourself out of the picture. But it does mean that you need to consider whether you are able to handle all of the work on your own or not. Working with a strategy planning team will ensure that you can grow more, that you can be on as many social media sites as you would like and still see results, and that your message, no matter where you send it out, is still going to be seen by the people who matter the most.

Once you have this team in place, make sure that you all come together and check that you are on the same page. You want to have regular meetings, even if it is just one or two people on the team, about what you want your message to say, where you want to post, if there are going to be any big events that are going to happen with your brand, and anything else that could be important for this process.

Other

There are a lot of people you can work with when it comes to ensuring that you are going to get the best out of your personal branding. This is not something that is going to happen overnight, and it can actually take quite a bit of time for you to see the results. Having a good team on your side to help you understand what needs to be done, to keep you on track, and to keep all of the plates spinning at the same time can be one of the greatest things that you do for your personal brand.

Depending on the type of personal branding that you are trying to do, it is possible that you will need a few other people on your side to ensure that you can get it all done. The number of people, and the job that they will have will all depend on what you are trying to do. If you decide to publish some workout videos, you may need to have a few people on your team to workout with you. If you are cooking, you may need some people to look up recipes, shop, and prepare the food for you.

This is where you really need to have a good strategy in place to help you get started with your personal branding. You need to make sure that you are able to pick out the right team to help you get the work done. You don't want to hire people for jobs that don't need to be done, and you don't want to hire too many people when you could, and should, do some of the work on your own. Knowing what your personal brand needs, and what you should have in place to make it work, can help make it more successful.

Creating your own personal brand is going to take a lot of work. It is going to take a lot of work and some time, you will find that having a good team behind you can make your personal brand more successful. You want to take some time to learn more about your brand, and what it will take to get it off the ground and running, and from there you can pick out the team that you really need to see the best results!

Chapter 9: Creating Your Personal Brand on Facebook

One of the first places that you an start on when it is time to create your own personal brand is through Facebook. This is a social media site where billions of people throughout the world have a profile, or use it in different ways. It is likely that a lot of the people you are targeting will spend some time searching for you on here. Being able to create a good personal brand on tis social media site can help you get further in your personal efforts.

When you are using Facebook to grow your personal brand, there are a few things that you need to consider. First, you need to define yourself. Try to figure out what your own personal brand is going to stand for. You should have a pretty good idea of how to do this from the other steps that we have talked about before. But taking some time to plan ahead so that you keep everything together, so that the story is cohesive, and so you are able to get the results that you would like out of this process.

Once you have a good idea of how you would like to define yourself, it is time to go trough and choose your friends carefully. You are trying to build up a brand, and come up with a new network that is nice and strong. You do not want to waste your time inviting anyone and everyone on Facebook to join you. It is important for you to carefully choose who you would like to share your information with, and whom you are "seen" with on this site. Make sure that you spend time interacting with those who your brand is built for. You can include people like future employees, colleagues, your boss, or clients you would like to attract to you.

Now you need to decide on your strategy. Just like a company will do when it is time for them to brand a new product, you need to come up with a good branding strategy as well. While it is possible for you to work on changing this up over time, it is a good idea for you to write out much of the strategy, and your plans, as possible. Think about where you would like this branding to go, what your branding will get you to in the future, and more. This can help you to know when you should post content, and what should be in the content, to really reach your target audience.

While you are working on creating your content, and getting it all set up, take some time here to change up your privacy settings. If you are serious about creating your own personal brand, then you need to take some time to filter out all of the content and information that you put out there. You have some choices here. You can choose to not let certain people see your profile. You can cut off certain groups, and more. Or, if you want to keep most of it private to the genera audience on Facebook, but you would still like a way to get others to come and look at your page, you can let some of the information be accessible to the public, or some of the ones you are not friends with.

Along these lines, make sure that you don't let out too much of your own personal information here. You want to talk about things that go with your brand, but telling everyone about all your problems, about the fight that you had with your spouse, and more, is going to harm the brand image that you are trying to come up with here. You can talk about things like your educational information, your successes, your work information, and anything that relates back to the personal brand that you want to create.

While you are in the settings, make sure that you turn off any of the tagging options on pictures. This ensures that you are going to be protected from malicious attacks, spam, and other things that could be unpleasant. In some cases, the issue could be with a good friend who didn't care that much about their internet presence, and they post something that could hurt your image or embarrass you. Turning this tagging feature off can help keep your page clear and prevents any of this happening.

Another option to work with is to create your own vanity URL. This is a domain that you can use on Facebook. This is basically going to take away all of those numbers and letters that Facebook automatically gives you and allows you to have a URL that is easier to recognize and use.

Since you are working on your own personal branding here, you will want to take some time to go through and fill in all of the professional details that you can. This is one of the neat things about Facebook because it will allow you to explain more about what you do in y our position, rather than just typing in the position of the company you are in.

This is a great way for you to take things a step further and really explain what you do in your position. You can talk about what your goals are in this position, even if you work as freelancing or are starting your own business, and it will ensure that you are able to differentiate yourself from some of the others out there are the market who may be doing the same thing. If someone else lists out financial advisor, but you have a full description about your duties, that is going to stand out.

Once your profile is all set up and ready to go, it is time to start doing the proper networking. This is meant to help you to increase the number of friends you have, and in return, this ensures that you are going to be seen by more people. You should spend some time engaging with the friends you already have on Facebook, produce and send out quality content on a regular basis, and import your contacts as they start to grow.

Posting is so important when you are working on your own personal brand. You are going to lose out on a lot of followers and friends, and your personal brand is never going to grow if you do not post updates and content on a regular basis. You need to post things that are interesting, things that are going to keep the interest of your friends, and will convince them to keep coming back over and over again.

First, you need to make sure that you are posting on a regular basis. This number is going to be different for each person, and you may find that what works the best for one person isn't going to work for you. Experiment a bit to see what seems to work the best for you. At least once a day is usually best. If you only post sporadically, your friends will have no reason to come back and check out the content that you are providing. But if you post every hour or more, this is just going to get annoying and people will stop as well.

You also have to pay attention to the things that you choose to post. You don't want to post things that have nothing to do with your personal brand, or the things that you want to showcase here. You want to make sure that it fits with your strategy, it fits with your personal brand, and that will catch the attention of your audience. You can post updates, you can post articles about the topic, and other information that helps you to promote the image that you want to your consumer.

The pictures that you post on Facebook can be important as well. While pictures are not as important on Facebook as they are on other social media sites like Pinterest and Instagram, you still can make good use of these in order to get the results that you would like. You should start out by putting up a profile photo that is professional and high quality. The picture that you choose is going to depend on what you are trying to promote. A young professional who is looking for a job is going to post a different picture compared to someone who is trying to do a new show on YouTube and wants to get noticed.

While we are here, make sure that you take special care of all the pictures that you post on your profile. Everything, whether it is the articles, the posts, and the pictures, need to fit in with the strategy that you set up before. You want it to all fit with the image that you are projecting to your potential consumer, and the pictures you choose can definitely do this. You just need to make sure that you are using them in the proper manner.

Next, you should link your Facebook page to some of the other social media pages that you are trying to do. This is going to help you to reach more people, and can raise some more interest in what you do, and in yourself in particular. The more people who visit your blog, or your other social media sites, will find that this cohesion makes you look more professional. If you find that across your social media pages, and anything else that you are using, that something doesn't end up matching together, it is time to work on it, or choose not to link it. You should also consider having the same e-mail or username address for all of the accounts so that you can keep the branding going among more than one account.

Once all of this is set up, it is time to consider running a new group or a new page on Facebook. If you already have quite a few friends on Facebook, you will be able to increase this number with the help of a new page. This is a great way for you to promote your personal brand, along with your interests and your business. When you make a group, you will be able to connect to more people. The people who are interested in the same interests as you, or who are on the same topics as your personal brand, will be able to find this page, and you will get some organic growth to your network and to your brand over time.

Once you are ready, you are able to work with Facebook events. You will be able to make your own event, or you can promote an industry event or gathering in that area. You can even use this kind of event to encourage your current friends and followers to come out and get more of their friends to follow you as well.

Make sure that any event that you choose to do is set up well, and is able to meet the needs that you have. if you are able to make it interesting, and ensure that it stays with the strategy that you already have, while fitting with that new brand that you are trying to grow, it can do some wonders for increasing your reach. It can even make your consumer and friends feel like they are doing something important, or like it is well worth their time in other ways.

There are a lot of different ways that you are able to grow your own personal brand. But one of the first places that you need to look at for doing this, mainly because of all the options and all of the people who are on this social media site, is Facebook. This chapter has the tips and tricks that you can use in order to take that personal brand, and get it to flourish when you use Facebook to help you to do it!

Chapter 10: Creating Your Personal Brand on Instagram

After Facebook, Instagram is a great online platform that can help you to get some of the following that you want for your own personal brand. This is a very popular photo uploading platform where you are able to post and share both images and videos.

As someone who is looking to grow their own personal brand, it is worth your time to look into Instagram. It currently has more than 150 million users, and more than 5 billion pictures uploaded. What this means is that this is a social network that has a very wide range of audience, whether they are real photographers who are using this, or just some of the general users to the whole thing.

But you will find that Instagram is so much more than just a social network that you can use. It has actually become one of the best platforms to use if you want to build up your personal brand. This social media platform has become a big market for individuals and companies alike who want to be able to build up their own personal brands, and it is easy to find a ton of celebrities who have gone on there and started to build up a brand as well.

This social media site is very full of images and videos and more. This means that, even though you are able to write some information with the pictures, you need to concentrate more on the visuals than anything else. The first thing that anyone is going to see is the pictures, and they actually have to go through the process of clicking on the picture before they even see any words. Working on high-quality images to help promote your brand is something that you will need to consider.

If you are interested in working with Instagram to work on your personal brand, you need to make sure that you know how to come up with high quality content. Some of the things that you can consider when it comes to creating your own personal brand on Instagram includes:

Go with a username that is unique

Many new brands on Instagram are not going to take the time to pick out a username that is unique. But since this username can help portray a lot of characteristics about your brand, it is important that you choose it wisely.

First, remember that you should not go with a username that is long and hard to remember. And don't go for one that your followers are not able to pronounce. If your followers aren't able to remember it, they won't. They will just give up and choose not to follow you any longer. With this in mind, you want to make sure that you go with a username that is easy to remember, simple, and easy for your followers to find.

If you plan on using more than one social media site to help promote your brand, it is helpful to use the same unique name for all of the handles. This makes it easier for your followers to find you, no matter what site they are on.

Build a unique persona

One of the big keys tat you will notice when it comes to building up your personal brand is uniqueness. Your exclusivity is going to create a favorable kind of opinion in the minds of others. There are a lot of ways tat you are able to do tis from your profile picture to the information that you present, and even with the postings that you choose to do.

Try to find ways that you can show off your brand, and even your personality, in the posts that you are doing. This is going to help draw more people in, and will make it easier for you to get the results that you want. The more that you are able to set yourself apart form others, and really showcase what makes you so special compared to the rest, the better you will be when it comes to growing that brand.

Working with hashtags

Hashtags are a great ting that you are able to add into your personal branding on Instagram as well. These hashtags are going to make it easier for others to search for you in the community. But for these to work, you need to make sure that you are working with tags that are searched quite a bit, and the ones that are popular. You will find that these hashtags are the smart way for you to reinforce your brand in a way that nothing else can. Users who don't really know much about these hashtags are going to make a story out of using a long list of hashtags, which comes out looking messy, and can turn your followers off.

Picking out the right hashtags can make a big difference in how successful that you will be with people finding your videos and pictures. Make sure that you do your research and find the ones that are going to match what your followers are looking for, and what works the best for your business.

One thing that can really help your brand to grow is to create and then promote your own personal hashtag. When you make your own hashtag, it is going to highlight your brand, and can help make it stronger. You need to come up with something that is unique, something that you know no other business or brand has, and something that will set you apart from the rest of the competition. Make sure that you put this unique tag on all of your promotional items, your pictures, and your videos and try to promote it with your followers.

Post images that are exclusive

You can also consider posting images that are exclusive These can be the ones that have just shown up on the web within a few minutes and you are one of the first to showcase these, or the pictures that you were the one to take. Generally photographers are going to be used in order to get these pictures set up, but if you are trying to build up a new brand on your own, then this is something that you would want to do as well.

No matter what kind of brand you are trying to build up, you should consider working with this idea. You can show exclusive items, pictures, videos and more, especially if you are only showing this information on your Instagram page, rather than on all the other ones as well. You will find that this is a great way to establish the brand that you want, and will help you to gain more followers over time as well.

Working on your profile

Your profile is going to be one of the first things that your follower is going to see when they get on Instagram. You want to make sure that this is going to be set up in a way that you are able to impress them. And, if you are able, you want the follower to know what your brand is all about as well.

When you are working on the information and the picture that is on your profile, you need to pay special attention. You want to choose a picture that is original, and high quality. Or, if you have a logo, you can put this on there as well. You want this picture to tell people what your profile is about. The information that you place on the profile needs to explain about your brand and what it is going to deal with.

With the right information, and some good pictures on the profile, you will find that it is easier for users to recognize your brand, and they will quickly be able to recognize what kind of updates they can expect to find on the page. If you want to, consider adding a bit more information so that your followers, or anyone who is interested in you. This can include your Facebook and Twitter account handles, your phone number, and your professional email address to make things easier.

Be careful with your tagging

Tagging can be something that helps you out a lot with your profile. But you do need to be careful with this. You don't want to just tag everyone you can find, because this means that you are going to tag people who are not supposed to be tagged. If you do decide to tag people, make sure that you are careful with who you place on the picture or the video. Only add them if they have approved, and if it makes the most sense.

Consider doing contests

Another option that a lot of people like to do when they start on Instagram, and when they want to work on their own personal brand, is to run contests. You can choose how often you would like to do this, including each week or each month. These are helpful in order to help you get more visitors to your profile, which can do wonders for how much you are able to grow your brand and become recognizable throughout the world. These contests are going to bring you a lot of results that are pretty impressive, including the ability to boost the productivity of your brand by 80 percent or more.

The way that you do this contest is going to depend on what works the best for you. You may make sure to offer up some prizes to the winners of the contest to entice them to help you out. But if you choose to go with the prize option, make sure that you actually give out the prizes. Many companies have ruined their reputations because they did social media contests and then never announced the winners or gave out the prizes that they had promised.

Tell a story

When someone comes to your profile, they should be able to see a nice story spelled out there. You want your videos and photos to tell the story of your brand. Your followers need to be able to sense this and find it all meaningful. Your users are always looking for something new and interesting so post something that is going to engage the user.

There are a lot of different stories that you are able to make, and it is going to depend on the brand that you are going to portray to others. You always need to make sure that you are impressing those who come to your profile, and that, when they look at the pictures and videos that you post, they will understand what your story is, and more about your brand. If your content is not doing this, then you are wasting a lot of time without building up your brand.

Work on quality

As you are working on your Instagram profile, make sure that you focus on the quality. Many people, especially when they are first getting started, will just focus on the quantity of posts that they are able to post. They don't spend time worrying about how good the quality is, and this is what can hurt them. Any time that you post one image or vide each day, you need to make sure that it meets the excellence that you need before you decide to post it.

You need to be careful with the images that you choose as well. You want the best ones to go with all the posts that you choose. And double check that it is the best one. Remember, all of these are going to portray your image to the outside world. If you post something that is low-quality and doesn't meet up with your brand, it is going to end up harming your personal branding. Make sure that the image and the vide are interesting and carries the ability to enthrall your followers.

Interact with others

One thing that you need to really focus on with your profile on Instagram is to interact with others. It isn't enough to just post a few pictures on the site and hope that others are going to start following you. There are millions of pictures found online, even on Instagram. You need to make sure that you are able to interact with others and make sure that you are forming some relationships with others while you are there.

First, if anyone comments on your pictures or your posts, then you need to try and reply back. This doesn't have to be instant as no one expects you to spend all of your time sitting at the computer and waiting for those comments to come in. Setting aside a bit of time each day to handle these comments and to reply to your followers can make them feel like you truly value them, and will keep them coming back.

You can also work on getting new followers to come to your page and get them to pay attention to you. Finding other pages, especially other personal brands, that you can follow will help. Commenting on pictures that you really like, following the right people, and answering questions, whether they are on your page or on another profile, can really make a difference in your reach, and who decides to follow you.

One note about commenting on other posts and profiles is make sure that they provide some value. Just replying "cool" "yes" "ok" or something similar is not going to work here. That doesn't provide any value. You should add in at least a few sentences to answer questions, and to help you to really provide some value to the others on that page.

Chapter 11: Creating Your Personal Brand on YouTube

YouTube is one of the premier video sharing website in the whole world. While there are thousands of different websites out there that you are able to use in order to try and improve your personal brand, there aren't any that will be able to give you both the reach, and the credibility, that are needed to make a big impact and to get people to notice you like YouTube. But if you would like to create your own personal brand, you need to make sure that you are using YouTube in the right manner. Some of the things that you should keep in mind when it comes to creating a personal brand on YouTube includes

Brand your profile

In order to make sure that you are able to build up a good personal brand on YouTube, you need to consider the best way to position yourself. If you already have a personal brand put in place on some of your other social media sites, then you can simply move it over to your YouTube channel as well. Some of the things that you need to consider when it comes to branding your YouTube channel and getting it all set up and ready to go includes

1. Choose a channel name: Depending on the branding strategy that you choose you use, you can use a unique show name, the name of your company, or even your own full name. Think about the name of your channel carefully as this is going to be the one that you are stuck with for some time.
2. Profile setup: You need to take some time to fill out your profile. This is going to make it easier for others to find you when they do a search. You can also upload an avatar and get that set up so that people can find you even better.
3. Information on the channel Most of those who start to market on their channel don't realize that there are actually a

few account types that they are able to choose. If you consider yourself an expert in the field (or you would like to become one), then you should select the Guru account style. This allows you to come in with a custom logo and makes it easier to add in links.
4. Customizing the channel: When you are ready, you can go and log into the account, and see how the channel is doing. You can then go trough and add in any customizations that you want. You don't want to go crazy with this one, but taking the time to update things and change them around if it meets with your branding can make a big difference.
5. Title and tags on the channel. If you think that there are some good tags that are going to reflect the content of your videos, then go ahead and add them in. Think these ones through because they are going to be critical in helping you to really get others to find your information.
6. Colors and themes In your account, you will be able to take some time to look for the colors and the overall look that will best align with what your brand is all about. Take some time to choose this to ensure it looks nice and cohesive with the rest of the branding that you are doing.

Create some good videos

You do not want to become that person on YouTube who puts up a video that is low quality, the one who just spits them out as quickly as possible in the hopes of getting some more views. There are millions of hours of video on YouTube, so you need to be able to get yourself to stand out from the crowd. And providing your audience with videos that are bad or low quality is going to get you in a lot of trouble.

Content is going to be king, and when you are on YouTube, the only way that you can truly be successful is to make sure that your content is truly worth spreading. This means that it needs to be really interesting or really funny in most cases. In addition to good content, you want to make sure that you have the right kind of equipment to get yourself started. Never put bad or low quality videos on your YouTube channel. You are competing against a lot of other people who are uploading videos and trying to get to the same group as you. If you don't meet the same quality as them, you are going to be the one who loses.

When you are creating videos for your YouTube channel, think about the brand that you want to promote, and what your audience might like to see. You are still catering to the same audience that you did on some of the other social media sites, even if they haven't had time to look for you here yet. You can then use these ideas to start creating some amazing videos that will not only attract your current audience, but will bring in some new consumers as well.

Promote your videos

When it comes to promoting on YouTube, things may seem a little bit scary. With all of that content already found on this channel, you may wonder how you are going to make your video stick out, and how you will make sure that your audience is actually going to see you. Often, the best way to start promoting your channel, and any of the videos that you have on there, is using the network that you already have.

For example, if you have some other social media sites, make sure to post when you have a new video up. If you use any blogging in this process or in your strategy, writing about a new video, and providing a link, can help. Once your own friends and followers see the video, and like and comment on it, it can help raise you up a bit, and it won't be long before others are able to find out about the amazing content that you produce.

You will find that spending some time on your YouTube channel, and making sure that it is high quality and able to handle all of the branding that you plan to do, can do a lot of good for you. Create high quality videos, add in interesting information to your profile, and work hard to promote your videos, and you will find that working with

YouTube can be one of the best ways to help build up your personal branding.

Chapter 12: Creating Your Personal Brand on Twitter

Twitter can be a great platform that you can use in order to promote your personal brand, but you may find that it is a bit trickier compared to some of the other options. You are only given 140 characters to show your message, and to make sure that you are able to really let your voice, and the voice of your brand, show up for others. This can be a challenge, but you will start to get the hang of it as you work on it.

If you have used the Twitter site for some of your own personal needs, you are probably used to some of the things that you need to do in order to get Twitter to work well for you. But when it is time to make this platform work for your own personal branding, things will need to be changed up a little bit. Some of the things that you can do in order to use Twitter to build up a memorable personal brand include:

Follow the leaders

When you first set up the handle that you would like to use on Twitter, it is time to start following some people. You should take some time to follow a few of the leaders on Twitter. It is best if you are able to find some of the leaders who are in your particular field first. This allow you to do some networking, and can give you plenty of chances to comment and ask questions, opening up the door to how many people will see you.

The beauty of using Twitter is that you won't have to go that far in order to discover the best way to be successful with marketing. You will be able to observe the professionals and see how they do it. You also want to take the time to follow anyone who is sharing a lot of content, and who seems to be on Twitter, and very popular on there.

Over time, in addition to observing some of these accounts and learning how they play the game, it is time to start engaging them. Influencers, just like anyone else, like to hear praise from someone else, so start out with this. Of course, make sure that you don't expect this to turn into a home run. But, if you find that over time, the influencer decides to start following you, or if they even mention you on their page, then this is a big score.

If you do take the time to directly reach out to the other influencer, see what you are able to offer to them in return for them helping you. For example, if part of your personal branding included running a blog, you could offer to mention them in one of your blog posts. This can help them with their reach, while you work on your own reach as well.

Work on the profile and your brand

You do not want to get on any social media sites and not take care of your profile, and make sure that it, and any content that you add to it, are going to work together with your brand. To start, make sure that you go through and work on your profile, just like we have talked about with the other social media platforms on this list. You want to make sure that there is a good picture, one that highlights what your personal brand is all about (please leave the cutesy pet pictures off unless you are a vet or a dogwalker), and fill in all of the information that is there.

Since you are only going to be given 140 characters to go with each post, you do need to be careful about how you are posting things and whether they go along with your own brand or not. You want to still keep the content fresh, and you want to post things that are useful to the audience. Following those influencers above will make it easier for you to really figure out the best way to do this and still get your message across.

Create some good content

If you waste your time tweeting negative things, rather than working on your brand, then it won't be long before you start to build up a negative personal brand on Twitter. You want to make sure that you are tweeting insightful and helpful content so that you are better able to grow your own reputation. There is going to be something in common between all of the Titter brands that are the most impressive and this is that they are gong to post a steady stream of content that is valuable.

One thing to consider is that you can't tweet enough. Of course, this doesn't mean that you should spend every second of every day posting on your profile, and you shouldn't make it your goal to post 100 times a day. but if you see that there is some positive engagement going on with your profile, then it is fine to keep on posting. Unlike some of the other social media sites, Twitter has some more openness when it comes to the number of times you interact and post on there.

The important thing to remember is that the quality that you post needs to be high, and you need to find your own rhythm. If you find that posting every hour, every few hours, or a couple of times a day seems to work for your schedule and for your personal brand, then go ahead and do this. You need to figure out what works the best for you.

Another thing to remember is that you need to come up with some of your own content. It is fine to use some curated content, especially if you feel that it is going to truly benefit your readers. But if you are really serious about getting your own personal brand built up, then you need to post some original content. In fact, the majority of your content needs to be original, or your readers are going to quickly get tired of paying attention to you.

Engaging

Twitter, like some of the other social media sites that you may use, is going to be a two-way street. If you take the time to reach out to others, then it is more likely that they are going to engage wit you. You don't want to just put out some content, whether it is curated or you came up with it yourself, and then hope that the readers are going to do all of the work. You need to be active on the community and do some of the work as well.

You need to make sure that you set aside a bit of time each day to reach out and engage with the tweets of your followers, as well as influencer you would like to build a relationship with. Whether you read through some of the tweets that interest you the most, or you look at a profile, you can then take the time to compliment the other person, ask a question, or do some other things that can form a better connection.

It is best if you are able to handle all of this response on your own. Some beginners think that this is all going to be too overwhelming for them to do on their own, and so they choose to hire this out and do some outsourcing. But all of the most successful Twitter entrepreneurs will agree that it is better to handle the responses on your own, rather than hiring someone else to do it.

Test and analyze

Twitter is a great social media site to work with because it is going to give you feedback that is almost instant. Depending on what you post and who is online, you will see how it performs almost right away. This is why it is such a good place to share a lot of content, especially if you would like to test it out.

Doing this lets you get a good idea of what is resonating the best with your audience, so that you know what works and what doesn't. you can then take this information and bring it to some of the other platforms that you are working with. If you would like to make sure that you can test out your material, and easily find it later, you should use hashtag to make this easier. This is also helpful when you would like to compare how a tweet with a certain hashtag did when it preformed against some of the others that they used as well.

It is always a good thing to test out the information that you are posting online. But with some of the other options that are out there, it can be really hard to know what is going to work until it has been out there for a bit. With Twitter, you are able to get some results in, in a short amount of time.

Decide if you want to outsource

When you are working on Twitter, you don't really need to worry about outsourcing at all. This is really a platform where you should put your own energy and do the work. And since it only takes about 140 characters or less to get the message out there, this isn't something that is going to take up a lot of your time.

When you are working on your own personal brand, and you have a lot of things on your plate to juggle at the same time, it sometimes is tempting to try and find some things that you can do to reduce all the work that you need to do. But with Twitter, as with a lot of the other social media sites that you will work with, it is best if you are able to do the work on your own. This ensures that your voice is maintained, and you get a closer look at your audience to figure out what they really like.

Twitter is a great tool that you can use in order to help build up your own personal brand, especially if you are working with a few of the other social media platforms as well. When you are ready to start adding Twitter to your toolbelt, make sure to check out some of the steps and tricks that you can use to be successful with this above.

Chapter 13: Your Personal Brand Over Time – Tips to Getting the Most Out of Your Personal Brand!

Now that we have spent some time working on personal branding and some of the things that you are able to do with this branding, it is time to take it to the next level. Remember, this personal branding is going to be something that is going to take some time, and a lot of effort to accomplish. but the results are going to be so worth it. When you are ready to start building up your own personal brand, and you are excited to see some of the best results with this, some of the tips that you can follow will include:

Be authentic

When it comes to branding yourself, being authentic is going to be one of the best things that you can do. But what does this really mean? As we mentioned earlier, it means that you need to be yourself. Everyone's got their own quirk. Being able to show this to the people who are watching you, and laughing right along with them when you do something funny or make a mistake, can be a great way to connect with your audience, and to keep them coming back for some more.

Blogging

We have not really had much of a chance to talk about this one in this guidebook yet, though we have mentioned blogs a few times. One of the best things that you can do when you are trying to build up your own personal brand is start a blog. This gets your information out there, allows you to share information with others that they will find interesting, and you can even turn it into a way to make money!

Blogging when you first start out can be a challenge. There are a lot of blogs, on almost any topic that you can imagine out there. But since most of them are not that interesting, and many people give up after a short time working on them, there is still some room for you to come into the market as well. You just need to have the right kind of dedication, and the right determination, to get into the mix and not give up.

When you want to get started with blogging, you need to think about a niche or a topic that you would like to write about, and one that will go with your personal brand. And then you need to get to writing. Make sure that your articles are the right length, usually at least 500 words, though going close to 1000 is often better because it provides you with more room to write out the information that you want to share.

You have to keep a few things in line when writing for a blog. First, you need to take the time to write on a regular basis. In the beginning, writing a post every day is maybe best, so that you can fill up the blog and get content on there right away. But after you have had some time to get some good articles on there, you can back off a bit. Be consistent though. Decide what schedule is best for you, and for your time, and then stick with it. Many people find that writing an article once a week seems to be the best.

The articles that you write on the blog need to be interesting, they need to all go together, and they need to be about something that your target audience is going to be the most interested in. You also want to add in the right keywords to the mix so that your target audience is able to find the articles and look them up when they need something about that topic.

This blogging can take some time. You need to gain some followers, and it does take time. You won't be able to get a ton of followers over to your blog when there are only five articles for them to look at. Writing on a consistent basis, and placing notifications about the blog on all of your social media pages, can help you to gain more followers the organic way.

After you finally have enough readers, you will be able to increase your personal brand some more. You may find that affiliate marketing is a good way for you to find the followers that you need and sell products. You can sell some of the products that you decide to make. It may take some time to make this happen, but if you are willing to put the time and effort in, it is a great way for you to create a nice personal brand, while being able to earn some money in the process.

Provide value to your audience

When you are able to provide value to your customers, it is going to make a world of difference. There are always going to be a lot of competition that comes with any kind of brand that you are trying to work with. This means that you need to be able to show the consumer why you are able to provide some more value compared to the competition.

Now, you need to take some time to figure out what that means for your brand. You need to figure out how you are able to take your brand, your product, and you, and make it stand out from all that the competition is abe to provide. This can be hard. But the sooner that you are able to figure this out, the easier it will be to get yourself to stand out.

Step out of the spotlight.

This one is going to seem like it is a bit out of the normal, and a bit different than we have been talking about so far, but being in the spotlight all of the time can take a big toil on your life. In addition, people sometimes need to miss you a bit so that they start to realize better how much they need you in their life. You don't want to step out for a long time, but if you leave it behind for a few days, or even a week, you may find that it brings a new level to your brand and is so effective in helping you to grow.

This is such a simple trick to work with, and it is going to benefit so many things in your life. First, you get a nice break. Social media is one of the best ways for you to grow your personal brand and to ensure that you are going to be able to make the money that you want. But sometimes, spending hours on social media a day can get exhausting and can drain you out. Taking the time off like this, even for a few days, can help you recharge, and may help you to understand how you need to make some changes to your strategy.

In addition, stepping out of the spotlight is going to make a big difference in how much your followers are going to stick with you. You don't want to go off for too long. There is so much competition, that if you go off the social media for too long, then someone will come in and take the vacuum that you leave behind, and you will need to start from scratch. But you will find that taking a few days off, or maybe a week, you will start a greater connection between you and your consumers, and this can help build up your brand quite a bit.

Be consistent

If there is one secret that you must stick with when it comes to doing well with your personal brand, it would be consistency. Consistency can mean a lot of things. It is not just about posting on social media each day. it is also about having a unifying brand look and messaging overall. So, how do we make sure that we are keeping with this consistency?

First, take a look at all of your social media profiles. Do they all look different, or the same? Some will tell you that you need to have a lot of variety with your content. But in reality, the more consistent that you are with your posts and your social media, the easier it is to grow your following.

Think of it this way, if you had a favorite pop singer, someone you followed all the time, and then they suddenly released a jazz album, it is likely that you are going to lose interest. This doesn't mean that the jazz isn't good, but it does mean that you preferred the original music that they created. This is the same kind of thing that can happen with personal branding. Your audience is going to fall in love with a specific way that you decide to present your content. But if you decide to start changing your tune, or you don't maintain that consistency between all your social media sites, then your consumer is going to jump ship.

Network

There is no way that you are going to be able to grow that personal brand if you don't take some time to network. You need to make sure that you are creating as many connections as you can, both online and in real life. Without these connections, it is hard to spread out the information about your brand, and the fewer people who are going to learn about you.

It is going to be really hard to brand yourself if you are not taking the time to put yourself out there to meet and interact with other people. There are a lot of ways that you can network to help grow that personal brand, and you need to take advantage of as many of these as you possibly can. You can start up a blog, go to that Meetup event, mingle with others who are at the same conference as you, grab some coffee with someone you have just met, post on social media each day, go to a group at the library, and just find ways to be involved. It doesn't matter if you meet someone new online or in real life, you will find that networking is one of the best investments that you can do for yourself.

Remember, the more chances that you get to interact with other people, the larger your network is going to become. While it is sometimes tempting to stick to a niche focused network, you will quickly find that the smartest thing that you can do is to expand into as many other categories as you can. You will be amazed at the people you can meet, and how their expertise, advice, insight and more can make a difference in your own personal branding as well.

Don't let your nerves or your shyness or anything else get in your way. and never get in the habit of saying that you are too busy to network. We are all busy. And we are all a bit nervous when it comes to meeting new people. But you will find that anyone who has ever been successful with personal branding will get out there and try to network as much as possible. And if you want to be successful, then you need to do the same things as well.

Be an expert in your field

No matter what field you decide to brand yourself in, make it a point to become an expert in that field. People like to listen to, and learn things from those who they consider experts in the field. So if you can find some way to position yourself as this expert, you already are ahead of the game.

Branding yourself can sometimes be hard when you aren't sure what your area of expertise is. every influencer has to find their own niche to work in, and from there, they can grow and become an expert. So, if you are working on selling tools in your online store, you want to make sure that the consumer thinks that you are an expert in carpentry, furniture design, or some other relevant niche that is going to help you to sell those tools.

Maybe you are going to sell car parts. If you do this, then you need to find a way to position yourself as an expert in the automotive industry so that you are able to provide value to that group of people. It doesn't matter what field or niche you are in, you will need to make sure that you become an expert in that niche, so that it is more likely that your customer will listen to you.

Another method that you can use that goes along with this is to look at building a brand, personal or otherwise, around the things that you are already an expert in. say that you spend ten years working in a hair salon. You could decide that your personal brand is going to be sharing ways to deal with hair issues while you sell a variety of hair products. You can do this with anything that you want, and it is a great way to show others that you really know what you are talking about, so they are more likely to purchase from you.

Amplify yourself

While we did talk a bit before about why it is so important to be yourself, and to be authentic, amplifying yourself is going to be like the second step to getting this done. In a world, especially online, where there is a lot of noise, it is hard for you to get yourself to stand out from the crowd. When you take the time to amplify yourself, you are going to take the essence of who you are, and then run wild with it.

Keep in mind that for this to work, you need to make sure that you are still authentic. You are not lying about yourself to impress others.

But you are taking what is special and unique about yourself, and then shouting it out to the world, so that they are more likely to hear you and take notice.

For example, if you like to be a big risk taker, you may decide to build up a nice personal brand about how you love to take risks. One idea to do with this is to create some content that shows you doing a ton of activities that are risky, and show you as a kind of daredevil.

In this case, you aren't just talking about how you are a dare devil, and you aren't asking others to take your word for it. But you are amplifying it by quite a bit and showing others how you went about and did all of this as well. This ensures that you are able to sell your product, and really showcase the things that you have in your personal brand. There isn't any lying in here. But you are making sure that others know the true you, and that it stands out in the crowd.

There are a lot of different ways that you are able to amplify yourself, and ensure that you are able to stand out from the crowd. It is all going to depend on the products you are trying to sell, or what you are trying to do with your personal branding strategy. But the trick here is to stand out, to make some noise, and to get others to notice you, without having to lie about yourself and look like you are a fake in the process. This is a fine line, but a sign of a truly effective and successful personal brander is able to stick with this.

As you can see, there are a lot of different things that you can do to make sure that your personal brand is able to grow. Standing out from the crowd is going to be one of the hardest parts of the whole thing. But if you are able to follow the tips above, you are going to see some great results in the process as well.

Thank for making it through to the end of *Personal Branding*, let's hope it was informative and able to provide you with all of the tools you need to achieve your goals whatever they may be.

The next step is to start your own personal brand today. You can work on creating some of the goals that you would like to meet, picking out the type of personal branding that you would like to work with, and even choose your niche. From there you can expand out to find a good mentor, figure out your audience, create a good team, and post up a lot of good content.

As we have discussed in this guidebook, it does take some effort and some time to make all of this happen. You do need to have the right kind of dedication to the cause before you can stand a chance of actually seeing the results that you would like with it. For those who think that they will be able to create their own personal brand in a few weeks, only doing a bit of work on the side, failure is going to come quickly.

But for those who are willing to seriously follow the tips and techniques that we talk about in tis guidebook, you will find that it is easier than you think to make your own personal brand, and to help yourself to stand out. In our modern world, there is a lot of competition to be heard online, but only a few are truly successful and able to make this work!

There are so many reasons why you would want to create your own personal brand. But no matter which method you are picking from, you still need to put in the hard work to make it into a reality. This guidebook took some time to explore how to create your own personal brand through setting goals, picking out a target audience, having a mentor to help walk you through it all, and how a good team can make all the difference

Once you have all of the things above assembled and ready to go, we moved on to some of the ways that you can start and grow your own personal brand. We focused on some of the main social media sites, including YouTube, Twitter, Facebook, and more, so that you can get a good idea of what is expected to get that personal branding started. Of course, you may not be able to put all your energy into each one of these, and may need to choose just one or two for your needs. And that is fine. As you read through this guidebook, you will quickly see (if you know your audience well) which one is going to be the best for you and for your personal brand.

Creating a personal brand can take some time, and you need to be willing to get in there and do the work that is required. You face a lot of competition, but if you are successful, the rewards are going to be so worth it. When you are ready to get started with your own personal branding, and you are ready to see what a difference it can make for you, check out this guidebook to help you get started!

Finally, if you found this book useful in any way, a review on Amazon is always appreciated!

© **Copyright - All rights reserved.**

The contents of this book may not be reproduced, duplicated or transmitted without direct written permission from the author.

Under no circumstances will any legal responsibility or blame be held against the publisher for any reparation, damages, or monetary loss due to the information herein, either directly or indirectly.

Legal Notice:

You cannot amend, distribute, sell, use, quote or paraphrase any part of the content within this book without the consent of the author.

Disclaimer Notice:

Please note the information contained within this document is for educational and entertainment purposes only. No warranties of any kind are expressed or implied. Readers acknowledge that the author is not engaging in the rendering of legal, financial, medical or professional advice. Please consult a licensed professional before attempting any techniques outlined in this book.

By reading this document, the reader agrees that under no circumstances are the author responsible for any losses, direct or indirect, which are incurred as a result of the use of information contained within this document, including, but not limited to, —errors, omissions, or inaccuracies.

Printed in March 2023
by Rotomail Italia S.p.A., Vignate (MI) - Italy